My Science Library

What is It Made Of?

by Amy S. Hansen

Science Content Editor:
Kristi Lew

ROURKE CLASSROOM

www.rourkeclassroom.com

Science content editor: Kristi Lew

A former high school teacher with a background in biochemistry and more than 10 years of experience in cytogenetic laboratories, Kristi Lew specializes in taking complex scientific information and making it fun and interesting for scientists and non-scientists alike. She is the author of more than 20 science books for children and teachers.

www.rourkeclassroom.com

Photo credits:
Cover © vadim kozlovsky, Cover logo frog © Eric Pohl, test tube © Sergey Lazarev; Page 3 © Emese; Page 5 © Poznyakov; Page 7 © Anton Albert; Page 9 © hans magelssen; Page 11 © photobank.ch; Page 13 © mypokcik; Page 15 © ZouZou; Page 17 © Carlos E. Santa Maria; Page 19 © tikona; Page 20 © ID1974; Page 22 © Anton Albert, hans magelssen, Carlos E. Santa Maria; Page 23 © photobank.ch, ID1974, Vasilius

Editor: Kelli Hicks

My Science Library series produced for Rourke by Blue Door Publishing, Florida

Library of Congress Cataloging-in-Publication Data

Hansen, Amy.
 What is it made of? / Amy S. Hansen.
    p. cm. -- (My science library)
 Includes bibliographical references and index.
 ISBN 978-1-61741-725-2 (Hard cover) (alk. paper)
 ISBN 978-1-61741-927-0 (Soft cover)
 1. Materials--Juvenile literature. I. Title.
 TA403.2.H36 2011
 670--dc22
                           2011003766

Rourke Publishing
Printed in China, Voion Industry
  Guangdong Province
042011
042011LP

www.rourkeclassroom.com - rourke@rourkepublishing.com
Post Office Box 643328 Vero Beach, Florida 32964

Everything I touch is made of something.

What is it made of?

I wear a coat made of **cloth**. Cloth keeps me warm.

I ride a bus made of **metal.** Metal is strong.

I sit at a table made of **plastic.** Plastic can be hard.

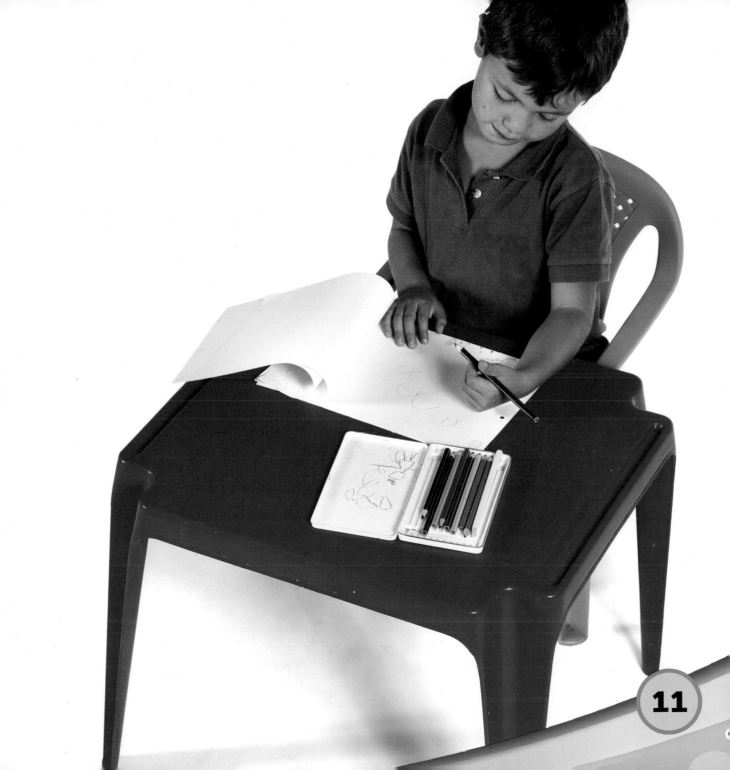

My hat is plastic, too.
Plastic can be soft.

I use a pencil made of **wood**. Wood can feel smooth.

I write on **paper**. It is made of wood, too. Paper rips.

I can touch the **playground.**

What is it made of?

SHOW what you know

1. What is the bus made of?

2. How does the wood feel?

3. Why does paper rip?

Picture Glossary

cloth (KLAWTH):
Cloth is a piece of fabric made from weaving or knitting pieces of thread or yarn.

metal (MET-uhl):
A material such as iron, copper, gold, or silver that is usually hard and shiny.

paper (PAY-pur):
Paper is a material made from chopped up wood, or from torn up rags.

plastic (PLAS-tik):
This is a material made by people. It is not found in nature.

playground (PLAY-ground):
An outdoor area where kids can play on swings, slides, and climbing things.

wood (WUD):
The material that makes up a tree's trunk and branches is called wood.

Index

Websites

www.textilemuseum.org

www.tryscience.org

www.strangematterexhibit.com

About the Author

Amy S. Hansen is a science writer who likes to figure out what stuff is made of, and how it is put together. She lives in the Washington, D.C. area with her husband, two sons, and two cats.